NEW WAY TO VOTE

To remove bad governance from a Country
and the misery associated with it!

Cid Adão
(Cidadão = Citizen)

Adão, Cid

NEW WAY TO VOTE

To remove bad governance from a Country
and the misery associated with it!

I DEDICATE THIS BOOK TO EVERYONE

who seriously strives to develop Civilization!

TABLE OF CONTENTS

FOREWORD

A SIMPLE AND PRACTICAL MODE FOR SAVING, MAKING EVOLVE, AND DEVELOPING ANY "DEMOCRATIC" COUNTRY OR ORGANIZATION EVEN IF BOGGED DOWN IN POLITICAL MEDIOCRITY!

"The world is a dangerous place to live, not because of those who do evil, but because of those who observe, and let evil happen, without doing anything".

Albert Einstein

IS THERE ANY "CRISIS" THAT IS NOT SIMPLY THE IDIOCY OF A PEOPLE WHO CHOOSE THEIR GOVERNORS INCORRECTLY?

To speak evil, to give up, and to be discouraged is very easy, but it does not change anything. Getting out of mediocrity is harder, but it can be done and often through something as simple as going to vote!

It is <u>a right and a duty</u> of the Citizen to vote for a party that has chosen Competent and Intelligent (and therefore honest) people for government, the only ones that can make a Country develop!

But some "killer" ideas may appear in people's minds:

The first "killer" idea: It is not worth voting because the candidates are all the same.

The second "killer" idea: I always voted for this party, I'm not going to change now.

How to overcome "killer" ideas: If the current party in governance is good, as it has developed the Country and cared for Citizens, vote for it again! If the current party in governance is not good, it is necessary that almost the entire population of the Country vote for another party, ***but vote wisely***, in order to force the current ruling party to disappear from the political scene!

How to do this: The book presents a simple and practical method, which is summarized in the figure of the cover that illustrates the process with a general summary table!!!

Any minimally intelligent person can see that Humanity is not taking advantage of the great possibilities that the development of technology allows to advance Civilization. On the contrary, mediocrity has spread all over the planet, and it seems that everything is sinking, from the destruction of the physical environment to the relations between people. The only thing that most people want is to have an increasing "number" in an account on the bank's computer! So, is there any admiration for the emergence of "crises"?

The greatest misfortune that can happen to a Country is that its people cease to be constituted mainly by thinking and acting people, and behave like a bunch of idiots who follow any "smart guy" who can convince them that manure is the same as gold. When this happens, the few wise people just want to shout, "I'm surrounded by donkeys." But then they remember that they too have been deceived in the past without realizing it and try to react positively, gaining courage and striving to advance Civilization.

To the question: Is there any way out? The answer appears: ***There is! <u>But there is indeed!!!</u>*** Although some may claim that there is no way out (those interested in maintaining the situation), in fact the situation can be changed, for the better, if most people wake up, think for themselves, and act right.

This book aims to pave the way for this purpose and to contribute to the advancement of Civilization, with the benefits it brings to everyone. (Even those who, in a situation of mediocrity, think that they profit from the murky waters gain from living in a civilized way, though they, foolish as they are, think that they profit more by walking in the murky waters.)

For example, there was in the past a Country that discovered new routes for Humanity: it surpassed what everyone thought was the end of the world! (Recalling what Einstein said, "Something is impossible only until someone doubts and realizes it!")

So now it is possible to create "new routes" of behavior to choose the rulers: this is the solution to get out of mediocrity and evolve for the better!

The Country referred to before, which, after a certain period of time, through the behavior of its inhabitants began to live in misery, can come out of the mud, recover its former name, and feel proud among other countries; at the same time its population can begin to live openly and unconcerned, if they start acting in such a way as to open new paths in the creation of Civilization, and then maintain the civilized situation they have created. Everything depends on putting in the government people who are Intelligent and Competent to deal with the interest of the Country! And the same can happen with any Country or organization where the rulers are chosen by voting!

It may be said that everything this book presents comes from the thought and experience of the author. It is the responsibility of the reader to identify the situations presented with real situations that he or she knows. It is also the responsibility of the reader to help create the reality in which to live! You can choose between one of the two options summarized briefly in (a) and (b) below:

a) Behave like a no-brainer (it means "having no brain" because that person does not want to think and act), letting others think for themselves and brainwash them with propaganda, thus becoming responsible for letting a Country (and consequently Humanity) sink, comforting themselves with the famous popular phrase,

"It's not worth it because there's nothing that can be done. Politicians are all the same crap". This thought arises from brainwashing they are receiving to maintain the state of things;

b) Begin to think and act on their own, so as to become responsible and active, then feeling the satisfaction of having done what they could to advance Civilization, the balanced behavior (the first step is to consciously vote) and to create a society that is good for all, putting in power not "crap", but Intelligent-Competent people to govern well!

**It's your choice!!!** and it has very important consequences!!! _**Never believe that your vote is insignificant!**_ A wise old man used to say, "If everyone carries away a small stone, they will have changed a mountain in the end!"

**It may not seem like it, but the solution is in your hands!!!**

I hope the ideas in this book can help you see clearly and choose wisely for the good of all!

Cid Adão (=Citizen)

INTRODUCTION

TO KEEP IN MIND WHEN READING THIS BOOK:

(and then apply at the time of voting)

"Only idiots continue acting in the same way and expect different results!"

Albert Einstein

"Something is impossible only until someone doubts, and realizes it!"

Albert Einstein

"Cleaning begets Cleaning; crap begets crap!"

Prof. Dr. Manuel Abreu Faro

Mediocrity attracts and promotes mediocrity; Competence attracts and promotes Competence. By what they do, not by what they say, it becomes clear to which group people belong. It is not indifferent to the future of a Country (or organization) to be governed by either type of person!

Adaptation of the previous

"If you are not interested in politics at all, sooner or later you will be governed by those who are less competent than you!"

Plato (B.C)

I know I look like a thief,
But there are many whom I know
Who without appearing to be
Are that which I seem!

Poet António Aleixo

"The Country lost its intelligence and moral conscience. Customs have been dissolved, consciences disbanded, characters corrupted.

The practice of life has only the direction of convenience. There is no principle that is not denied. There is no institution that is not mocked.

There is no respect for one another. There's no solidarity among Citizens. No one believes that public men are honest.

Some happy moneylenders explore. The middle class is progressively debilitated by imbecility and inertia. The people live miserably.

Public services are abandoned to a dull routine. (...)

The State is considered in its fiscal action as a thief and treated as an enemy. (...)

The certainty of this indignity has invaded our minds.

Everywhere we go we hear: "the Country is lost!"

Eça de Queirós 1871

THE STRUCTURE OF THE BOOK

This book is composed of three parts:
- this introduction, which outlines the subject of the book;
- an interview with Cid Adão (Citizen), <u>which presents a practical and effective way of freeing a Country</u> from the "mediocrity" that is governing it, if that is the case;
- a long-term proposal on how to make Civilization grow and remain in any Country, or "democratic" organization, <u>so that its inhabitants live with the highest standard of living possible and enjoy living</u>. It is the system I have named ***Aristodemocracy***!

THE GOVERNORS OF THE PAST

I have always wondered why, looking at the history of mankind, only rarely were people governed by the most competent and dedicated people. Rulers were almost always the biggest criminals, the most abnormal, the "smart" lie specialists, or those who belonged to the elite and promoted mediocrity that governed the peoples.

And more: *The best members of Humanity, who are not usually the ones who govern, were almost always assassinated by those whom they tried to help.*

Even so, something amazing has happened: Humanity has continued to evolve! But it could have been at a much higher level of evolution and Civilization, and people could have lived much better, if governance were done by people competent and appropriate for the role of governing!

This book presents a simple and effective process of accelerating the development of Civilization by making the most competent and honest people be the rulers of nations. Then, as "Cleaning begets Cleaning ..." the same will happen in other organizations in the Country!

But this will not happen by a miracle. As I said before, it takes the action of each one, even of the one who thinks he or she is insignificant. The starting point is to have the small inconvenience of going to vote well, if you live in a so-called Democratic regime.

THE REVOLUTIONS

Sometimes one hears that it is necessary to have a revolution. Having revolutions never served anything but to change one type of bad governance to another type of bad governance that is the same or worse than the previous one. Even the name means "a turn" and "return" to the same. Have you ever heard someone say, "The trough is the same, only the pigs have changed"? See for yourself. Observe, with eyes to see, what happened to the revolutions you know about. You can take as an example the case of your Country if there was ever a revolution in it.

I know a Country where there was a revolution and moved from "dictatorship to democracy". At the time of the revolution there was a Country next to it that was less developed, but it was fortunate to have no revolution and now also lives in "democracy" with a much better standard of living than the standard of living in the Country where there was a revolution.

Do countries need "individuals" who bring revolutions, *or thinking people to choose intelligent and competent rulers who bring "Evolution"?* Decide for yourself!

WILL I BE SURROUNDED BY DONKEYS?

See if it is not true that in the so-called "democratic

system", any "individual," as long as he succeeds in lying effectively, can become prime minister or have another position of governance for which he has no competence, thus sinking the Country or organization that he rules with disastrous consequences for all. Is it not the current situation, in the present "democratic system" that even the most mediocre individual can manage to lead a party? And this is because the intelligent and therefore honest people (the only ones who advance Civilization) do not act by " trickery" and are not experts in fraud, and therefore do not get involved in such schemes! However, the experts in the scheme are only able to work in murky waters and therefore need to keep the Country or the organization in these murky waters. And this situation will continue as long as people do not think for themselves and continue to go after "carrots," creating that famous environment that would make the boy in the tale "The Emperor's New Clothes" scream, "I'm surrounded by donkeys."

Do you not think that it is better to think for yourself and not just to believe what they tell us? Is it not good not to want to belong to the "donkey club," but to belong first to the group of civilized people and promoters of Civilization? And then does not everything start to change for the better?

THE GREAT ADVANTAGE OF CURRENT "DEMOCRACY"

In the initial democracy of ancient Greece all the people participated by voting on the decision that was to be taken on the subject under discussion. This is how the great philosopher Socrates was condemned to death. As we can see, it was a regime of governance that did not work and that disappeared, but it left the seeds that gave rise to the current "democratic regime" which for the time being seems to be the best until the "Aristodemocracy" system presented in the last part this book is implemented.

It seems to me that one of the major shortcomings of the so-called "democratic regime" is that voting is done in parties, not in intelligent-competent people. And in this situation any incompetent or "smart guy" who manages to get to the top of a party, usually by dubious means, can become prime minister and then name others like him, sinking the Country (... crap begets crap!).

Thus, it seems to me that the regime that is currently called "Democracy", although it can serves to choose the party that will govern, *has as its main advantage*, not the choice of who will govern but the possibility of removing from governance the "governing garbage" that sank a Country, if that has happened. *For this, it is necessary that almost all the people vote, but vote well*, and do not wait for others to decide or act, let alone sit idly by waiting for better days, as illustrated by the following case:

> "Father, your mustache is on fire!
> I know, my daughter! Do you not see that I am waiting
> for the rain to put it out?"

The possibility of voting to change the political system is such a simple but very powerful activity because it opens the door to change for the better and allows us to follow new paths for the progress of Civilization!

I alert the reader now to a deadly thought (the first "killer" idea) that causes many people not to vote, and it is summed up this way: "Why go vote if the politicians are all the same?" Won't this deadly thought be fostered by those who want to keep the current situation of mediocrity, preventing people from voting? (in order that they "continue to be there"!) We will deal with it later.

TO GIVE "NEW WORLDS TO THE WORLD"!

Extending our horizon to what is happening outside the Country, see if it is not true that if the people of a Country apply what is presented in this book (which is so simple), besides getting to advance their Country, will open paths by bringing in (do not forget that "Cleaning begets Cleaning ...") new paths of Progress and Civilization for other Countries of the whole world (where Humanity is letting itself sink in mediocrity and self-destruction)! The Country will thus start to open paths for a civilized future by providing a service... and a great service, to Humanity! (Do you not think this is needed?)

ACKNOWLEDGMENTS

I am very grateful to all the people who have been careful to read the book and to give me their opinion and suggestions, with particular emphasis on Professor J.C.L.! Thanks also to the Classic Publishing House for allowing the use of the cover for the print edition!

A very special thanks to Marsha Daigle-Williamson who did a review and optimized the text in English!

INTERVIEW WITH CID ADÃO (Citizen)

START

Journalist: Good Morning

Cid: Good Morning

Journalist: Before we begin our conversation, I would like to thank you for making yourself available to spend some of your time to talk about how to make a Country evolve and offer a better life to its Citizens.

Cid: It is always a pleasure to be able to talk with someone interested in developing a Country and to exchange ideas with those who seek to act correctly, rationally, and honestly, thus contributing to the development and progress of a Country.

Journalist: Thank you. It is always good to know that we are not alone in good causes. It has always made me very confused to see cases of two countries side by side: one is highly developed and continues to develop, while the other is still in the prehistory of development and is sinking more and more! Is this the result of chance, or do the Citizens of a Country have the real possibility of making their Country evolve?

Cid: The situation of misery you describe may be the effect of a dictatorship government, which is easy to verify by those who have been in countries dominated by dictatorial regimes. But when it happens that both countries have democracy, the situation you describe is usually due to the fact that the Citizens of the underdeveloped Country do not see that they are being deceived by experts in lies and thus continue to sustain political parasites that suck and destroy the Country instead of developing it.

Journalist: So, in order not to waste time, let us immediately move on to the fundamental subject of our conversation: is it possible, or not, in a Democracy like the one that currently exists in most countries, on the one hand, to detect and remove bad political parties and, on the other hand, to detect and maintain good political parties in order to advance the Country?

Cid: It is possible, and there is a simple, practical, and effective process for this. However, I must say that this type of party-based democracy does not seem to me to be the ideal system to choose the rulers of a Country, *because the main issue is not the type of party but the people who will govern the Country.* I have developed, therefore, another process for the choice of rulers, which seems to me to be much better than the present one, and which I have called "Aristodemocracy" (discussed in part 3 of this book).

Journalist: And what does this unusual word mean?

Cid: "Aristo" comes from the Greek and means "the best"; democracy also comes from the Greek and means "government by the people". I have brought the two together to mean that in this regime of "Aristodemocracy" the people choose their government among people who have shown, since they were young, that they are honest and the most competent for a given function.

Journalist: Then, if you do not mind, could you explain in more detail this system of choice of rulers? Now I was somewhat excited because it seemed to me that it is always possible to have a Country recover by removing it from the mud in which it has sunk up to its neck by successive governments of mediocrity and that makes it "always in first place", but unfortunately *only* when is counted starting from the end of the classification list.

Cid: It is always possible and even relatively easy if a large number of people in this Country want to think for themselves and act as the Citizens that they are. It is necessary that the population of this Country begin to act as conscious Citizens. If a lot of people are not worried about getting out of the mud where they are stuck up to their necks, but they are just worried that other people not make waves in this mud so they can breathe, then nothing can be done: the Country will continue in misery.

Journalist: So the problem cannot be solved by a narrow group of people?

Cid: The main responsibility ends up falling on a narrow group of people, the so-called rulers, who make the decisions that sink or advance a Country. But when you live in Democracy, in its current shapes, the choice of these rulers depends on the party for which people vote, a party that will later propose these rulers. So there has to be a large majority of conscious Citizens who vote together to keep the party that has chosen competent people to govern well, or to remove from the political map the party that has ruled badly, as will be explained next. So all the Citizens are called to collaborate in this process.

Journalist: So Democracy may not be the ideal political system?

Cid: For the development of a Country, Democracy, in its current shape, can be, or may not be the ideal system. As I said before, it all depends on the rulers and not on the party itself! And I have also told you that there is another process of properly choosing the appropriate rulers, the "Aristodemocracy," which seems to me to be a much more effective system than the current one. However, Democracy, as it is understood today, has a great advantage over dictatorial systems if Citizens do not get carried away in "songs," or turn Democracy into a regime of stupid people who always vote for the same party or for the parties that have sunk or are sinking a Country.

Journalist: And what is this advantage?

Cid: The great advantage of Democracy in today's situation is to be able to remove from the government the incompetent who have ruled a Country poorly, or to maintain in government a party that has chosen rulers who have governed well and made the Country progress. As you see, the main advantage of Democracy is not that the Citizens choose the rulers, because most of the time, these rulers are neither directly known to the Citizens nor is their mode of action known. Citizens vote for a party, and it is the party that is responsible for the choice of rulers. The whole point in the subsequent elections is to keep this party or "throw it in the trash" because of the way the rulers chosen by the party ruled the Country!

Journalist: And what happens when the population is asleep and continues successively to elect parties with politicians who deal only with the lives of their members and what they call their "political career," as well as the lives of family members and friends, the way it is usually said: "They are governing themselves instead of governing the Country"?

Cid: Well, in this case you will fall into an environment of established and promoted mediocrity that turns the Country into a muddle of corruption and causes the Country to sink in the path of misery. The Democracy is turned into the regime of stupid people.

Journalist: I now remembered a phrase I had heard in the past and that said more or less this: "Cleaning begets

Cleaning, crap begets crap. By the results of what people do, one can distinguish the people who belong to each of the two categories ".

Cid: It's a great truth, as you can see in everyday life. Each attracts and promotes its equal, creating majorities of "Cleanliness" or "mediocrity" that will later influence the evolution of a Country or any organization.

Journalist: So what will happen in an environment of mediocrity?

Cid: In an environment of mediocrity, "The one who knows... knows; the one who does not know ...is boss." Jobs and promotions are obtained, not by the competence and seriousness of the candidates, but by belonging to the "party" or "group" that was left to take over the power. People are always afraid "that colleagues will stick a knife on their backs" and the "trick" reigns. There is no company, institution, or Country that progresses with an environment like this: it self-destroys and, in the end, even the scammers who "climbed up" through tricks, are in the mud too, or end up being shot.

Journalist: And in an environment of competent people?

Cid: There, the rules are set by competent people so as to make the organization evolve and these rules are met naturally. Ethics is fundamental. Every person knows their place and is promoted only to a position that is within their capabilities! The work developed by each person is recognized, and so they are all satisfied. The company, institution, or Country walks "with the wind at their back" in a "clean" environment. Everyone wins with this, even the mediocre ones, who in the other system of "crap" would be bosses; now they gain more and they are more satisfied although not having, in this clean system, any place of prominence. This institution or Country has a high standard of living, and it is a pleasure to live there.

Journalist: But isn't such a scenario a "utopia"?

Cid: To tell a caveman that one could go to the moon was to provoke, beyond great laughter, the question that you put me. Likewise, although present-day Humanity has evolved enormously in scientific and technical terms, in terms of Civilization does not it seem to you that present-day Humanity is still practically in the time of the cavemen, destroying others and destroying itself? From time to time people appear as lights of Civilization, but instead of being taken advantage of, they are destroyed by the mediocre ones, for they reveal the mediocrity of those who seek to appear to be civilized. Humanity thus loses a chance to take a leap in Civilization. I remember, as an example from the last century, Martin Luther King.

Journalist: It is not easy, therefore, to create a civilized environment!

Cid: What is curious is that the task will even be easy if we consider it possible and try to perform the necessary actions, but it will be difficult if we consider it difficult or impossible. That is why mediocrity specialists try to keep others low on a cultural level and not to think for themselves, filling their heads with propaganda. And the first step for Civilization to progress is very simple: to have the slightest inconvenience of going to vote properly!

Journalist: But progress also does not "fall from the sky"!

Cid: Of course. It will always require effort, and from the beginning it is necessary to have the courage to recognize that it is possible to bring about the evolution, even when having to go against the general opinion that "there is nothing that can be done." In a democracy, the ultimate responsibility lies with the people who either did not vote or voted poorly. That is why it is also said that "a people has the government it deserves."

Journalist: So the process involves each Citizen being a person with his own thinking, guiding his life to advance Civilization by voting for a party not emotionally but rationally?

Cid: Yes. One of the main obstacles to progress is whether the Citizen is a no-brainer (meaning unable to think for himself), or votes emotionally (because he has always voted for that party, either because his father also voted for that party or because he thinks that his party is very good, even if it has sunk the Country). These kinds of people just repeat what is in fashion; they clap their hands because others do, even if they do not agree. Then there are parasites that suck the society dry, usually political parasites or people attached to them, and instead of being removed and "sent to work," they are applauded by this type of acephalous people, which continues the idea of being the best because others applaud them (while, at the same time, the society or the Country is sinking).

Journalist: This reminds me of a very funny story that you told me one day about a dog and its parasites. Would you mind repeating it for the readers?

Cid: It is the story of a skillful tick that managed to convince a dog to move away from the house where he lived well and leave the care of his owner, because leaving home was "what was good for the dog"—to do what he had in mind without regarding the consequences, to have adventures without rules, to be as rude as possible—"this was freedom." So the dog moved away from the owner who treated him and kept him clean of parasites, giving him adequate food at the right times, vaccinating him (which caused him pain, and he, at the suggestion of the ticks, began to think the owner was wicked). It is evident the dog began to languish and to feel bad. On the other hand, the ticks were fattening themselves "without giving it any thought", spending time in "political meetings" to agree on what the best way was to persuade the dog that it was crucial for him to continue to maintain this tick-feeding lifestyle. And even more, they managed to convince the dog that they would still do him the favor of sucking him!!! And the dog remained very grateful to the ticks for the "revolution" they made in his life, while he was undone in misery!

Journalist: It seems crazy, but as I think a bit, the situation is not so unusual in the day-to-day of societies. The "ticks" have no interest that the "dog" thinks for itself and finds a way to live a civilized life, in balance and abundance ...

Cid: That is why conscious Citizens are fundamental in a Country and should be almost all the people of this Country, if they want to live well, that is, in a civilized way. Have you seen what would happen to the ticks if the dog began to think for itself, and returned to civilized life and to the care of his owner? As I said before, the curious thing is that this possibility is perfectly in your hands (or in your "dog leg", if we are in the story) and that it is very simple. *First*, the "dog" itself has to wake up and decide. *After that* he has to stop discouraging himself and start acting, taking the step of removing the ticks and going back to his owner, or looking for a new owner, always attentive and with "eyes wide open" so that the relatives of the ticks do not come to him, always disguised as indispensable friends, and lead him back to the life of misery to be parasites in him.

Journalist: Then there is the problem of recognizing who is "the friendly owner" and who is "the tick"!

Cid: The solution is very simple: with "the friendly owner" the dog progresses! He lives clean and is satisfied, with a good standard of living on a par with the other civilized dogs in the neighborhood. With the ticks, the dog is always in a miserable state where nothing works well. It also helps to detect a government of "ticks" if its members or the people attached to them appear with wealth whose source is unknown but could not come from the salary they have, because as the proverb says, "Whoever sells goatlings and has no goats... has found them somewhere." Recalling the phrase quoted above, "For the results of what they have done is what distinguishes those who belong to Cleanliness and those who belong to crap."

Journalist: And often this "dog" even consoles himself saying that he is not the only one that is miserable.

Cid: Yes, but what he should do is to compare himself with those who live well, striving to reach their level of Civilization, and not to stay at a lower level with the poor excuse that the "dog" gives, instead of acting to progress. I will tell you an anecdote to illustrate the situation:

At an international congress of medicine, a doctor from Country "A", a very civilized Country where people live well, states, "Medicine in my Country is so advanced that we can do a brain transplant, and in 6 weeks the patient is able to seek employment";

A doctor from Country "B," also civilized, but not wanting to be behind, says, "In my Country, we transplant a heart and in 4 weeks the patient is ready to look for a job";

Finally, a doctor from Country "C" (the backward Country, analogous to the "dog" with ticks) says with an air of mourning: "That is nothing !!! We have voted over and over again for unsuccessful rulers, putting "smart guys" in the government, well-spoken men who have never done anything in life and, after a short time, the whole Country has been looking for a job ".

Journalist: This reminds me of a Country that I know and which, sadly, has had several of these rulers, because the people insist on voting badly or not going to vote, and now it is "in crisis," in the mud, when it could instead be well.

Cid: As you can see, the main problem is very simple: every Citizen checks whether or not his Country is well governed. Then it simply suffices, after this, to alter or to maintain in government the party of the present rulers. And, <u>most importantly, one should never refrain from voting</u> because abstention can become the main cause of a Country's sinking into mediocrity.

Journalist: And how do you know if a Country has been well governed, when each party says that it has governed well, or that promise good governance in election campaigns if people vote for it? But then it looks like they're all the same and people get disillusioned and do not go to vote.

Cid: Any propagandist can say whatever he wants. This does not change the reality of the Country! But unfortunately, there are many fools who still "march to the same beat" and vote for the same party even when it is clear that they ruled poorly previously. With fancy talk one can prove that the worst war was necessary and even a benefit for Humanity. Of course, those who talk like this were never there and we cannot change fools. What is needed is that the majority of the population does not stop voting, and when they vote that they vote to maintain a party with good governance or to clean out the rubbish that sank a Country! *And this is easy to verify: we feel it in everyday life.*

Journalist: So the current situation of a Country is what shows whether there was good or bad governance.

Cid: Yes. It is said that "against facts there are no arguments".

Journalist: But each party usually paints a very black picture of the other parties and a very colorful picture regarding itself.

Cid: There are many experts in the scheme, as well as many good actors in politics, and if we let them act, they are the ones who get "to move up" and to have the leading positions in an environment of established and promoted mediocrity. But there are four "basic touchstones that immediately show whether a Country has been and is being well or poorly governed. The Conscientious Citizen observes them, verifies if he has been well treated by the parties that have already been in the government, and chooses the party for which to vote, according to his observation without being influenced by "electoral songs". It also helps to note that good rulers govern with a concern to develop the Country, and bad rulers are anxious to win the next election, filling their own pockets and the pockets of their friends, appearing in grand openings and making great promises in the election year, as what we can classify as "the electoral puppet."

Journalist: And what are these "basic touchstones"?

Cid: They are: Education, Justice, Health, and Social Security.

Journalist: What about the economy and the welfare of Citizens?

Cid: If the "basic touchstones" are assured, the economic level increases steadily because the infrastructures are created for their development and people begin to live better.

Journalist: Can we then look at each of them in greater detail?

Cid: For sure!

Journalist: So let's start with Education.

EDUCATION

Cid: Mediocrity is very afraid of educated and learned people. In a Country governed by mediocrity, although much is said about fostering the quality of education, what they want is for people not to be educated and to have a low level of knowledge. You know, "In the land of the blind the man with one eye is king," and education gives two eyes to people. Thus, people can see that "the Emperor has no clothes" and needs to be replaced so as not to "undress" the Country as well.

Journalist: When you talk about education, does you refer to education about the way people should act when they meet with each other or to the training and knowledge people gain at school from childhood?

Cid: The two are interconnected and complement each other, so it is necessary to speak of both. And this subject of education is a crucial subject for the development of the Country.

Journalist: We can then start by the education of people when they meet in their daily lives.

Cid: It's ok. Have you noticed that in a civilized Country people are naturally educated and respectful when they meet, living harmoniously, while in a Country ruled by mediocrity, besides holes in the roads and garbage on the ground, people are naturally coarse and false, always lurking to see if the other (even their best friend) falls, so they can laugh at and mock him?

Journalist: Since you talk about it even in the media you notice it. For example, I have already noticed that on television in a Country governed by mediocrity, any "boy" who works as a journalist addresses the people who could be his grandparents with the familiar "you", with a total lack of respect, while they should be called "Mr. So-and-so, "or" Mrs. So-and-so," with all due respect.

Cid: Unfortunately it is so. Even when they refer to those who hold the highest positions of government, they refer to them as " Joseph has come ..." instead of "the President of the Republic has come ...". It is absolutely incredible what a low level one can arrive at when one lets mediocrity rule.

Journalist: There we go back to that phrase "crap begets crap ...". In a civilized Country, such a journalist might not even get a journalist job, or be such a sad figure.

Cid: Of course. Even if it unfortunately happens, because of the voters' lack of vision, that the President of the Republic people voted for is a "pebble with two eyes", that person still represents a position of extreme importance for the society, which is the reason he has to be treated with due respect.

Journalist: But the President of the Republic, as well as the other political office holders, also have to respect the Citizens!

Cid: That is another indicator related to education: the way governors behave. In a civilized Country the rulers and party members respect each other and respect the laws and the rest of the people. In a Country of political parasites, they think of themselves as superior beings (and they are: superior in mediocrity!) while at the same time they regard others as second-class beings who are only useful to elect them (and to pay for their privileges).

Journalist: They even told me that the top leader of a Country publicly demeaned the Forces of the Order simply because they had been mistaken on the way. It is a public shame for this Country to have such a leader, and now I see how this can serve as an indicator of the governance capacity of the party to which he belonged!

Cid: That's right, but he still holds the position of leader.

Journalist: Yet such people only embarrass a Country. They should never have been elected to such offices.

Cid: And in a civilized Country they would never be. Once again we return to the main problem in our conversation: to find out what indicators can inform us of the party's governance capacity, in order to avoid "mediocrity" governing a Country, and if it already happened to govern, to remove it from governance, quickly and definitively, in the next elections.

Journalist: We can now move on to the so-called school

education, or academia.

Cid: It is very easy to see if a Country has been well or poorly governed in this area. It is enough to observe what is happening with the students, because the concern of a serious government is to support and develop good students, as well as to create the conditions to foster a teaching of exigency and quality so that all the students can have a good formation. That is: it aims high and really stimulates excellence, which is what is needed in developing the Country.

Journalist: And how do you distinguish a government of mediocrity in this area?

Cid: It is distinguished by verifying if its education policy generates a Country of "donkeys". The concern of such a government is only to maintain a good image, artificially avoiding what they call school failure. They are the same "donkeys" that maintain the rulers who motivated them. Thus, they tolerate a lower level: bad students pass from one level to the next (to give the appearance that everything is well with the so-called "school failure" and to avoid problems with students' parents), teachers almost have to ask the students to let him teach classes; the students who are considered heroes are the most uneducated, or those who break the school windows with rocks (they are called "the irreverent ones"). You are seeing the beautiful burial of the Country that has such politicians as rulers and such students as future rulers, or coworkers at work (crap begets crap ...).

Journalist: Some weeks ago I was amazed because I saw on TV that there were parents who had been waiting in a queue for more than a day to enroll their children in a certain school so they could give them a quality education! And this was almost one year in advance for the beginning of classes. So there are still parents who are concerned about giving their children good education..

Cid: It is easy for me "to guess" that such a school is a private school and that it is independent of the Government.

Journalist: And you are right!

Cid: This only shows how it is possible to offer a good education and therefore it is also possible in public education. There are teachers and parents interested in this! Again the problem lies with the rulers and in the support given to the schools by the Public Ministry. If in some private schools one does well, one can also do well in public schools and with more reason. Thus, if parents are concerned, they need to vote adequately to clean up "mediocrity" and elect serious rulers who foster education.

Journalist: So, in order to verify whether a government was competent in the area of education, it will suffice to ask: did these rulers create an education aimed at the formation of good students and the creation of conditions in schools in order to generate good students and good Citizens or did they create and allow conditions in schools that let mediocrity prevail, lack of respect and appreciation of the "smart guys"?

Cid: Yes, it's very simple, just check that! It is enough to see what happens concretely in the schools where their own children attend, or the children of the rich and famous, as well as to be attentive to what social communication shows of the Country in this area of education. Then, at election times, take note of this aspect to choose the party to vote for, as we will see later.

Journalist: But in universities, teachers will be aware of what is going on and try to correct it.

Cid: The competent teachers, yes, but if most are on the side of mediocrity, they are also sinking with the Country. Do not forget: "Cleanliness begets Cleanliness ..." I was told by a mediocre professor who left the University where he was, that he went to another where a relative, who was the Rector there, arranged to make him a Full Professor. In the south of the Country there was a new University lacking professors, so he said "good-bye" to the university where he was (including his relative) and moved with his wife to the University in the south, where of course they arranged a way to employ his wife.

Journalist: In this way he also got to be the Rector of a University!

Cid: But he really did! And now what do you think was fostered at this University while he was Rector: mediocrity or Competence?

Journalist: It is not be very difficult to guess: in an organization of mediocrity ...

Cid: When they told me about this sad case (and there were situations of plagiarism, etc.), to me it was perfectly demonstrative of the famous phrase "mediocrity attracts and promotes mediocrity, competence attracts and promotes competence". So do not think that universities are safe in a Country where mediocrity reigns. If the Country's voters continue to maintain mediocrity in government, the problem will continue to grow in all institutions.

Journalist: As for Education topic, I am enlightened. Let us then go to Justice topic.

JUSTICE

Cid: Justice is another of the basic pillars in the development of a society. Justice in a Country is not only related to the courts, but also to all the security forces that deal with the protection of each Citizen.

Journalist: Then can we also verify the governance capacity of a particular party by the way it administers justice in a Country, which is easily detected by checking, for example, if people are safe to go out at night without being robbed?

Cid: That is an example, but there are more things to check. In a civilized society "Justice is blind" to the kind of people involved in a process and treats all people the same way. In this type of society the judges also have little to do given the civilized state of the Citizens; only very rarely is a case brought to justice, and therefore, the cases in the courts are few and are quickly and dignifiedly resolved. In this type of society mediocre judges are also held accountable for fraudulent judgments and removed from the magistracy.

Journalist: And in the society of mediocrity?

Cid: In a society of established and promoted mediocrity, many judges sell themselves, the results of the trials depend on the people involved, and several judges get fat on lunches and dinners with influential and well-heeled people (often their wealth comes from money illegally obtained). The courts do not have the conditions to operate well, and the number of cases is growing; they accumulate, dragging on for years and years without any resolution, and the judges can make the blunders they want with impunity because they are untouchable.

Journalist: Therefore, in this case, the Citizen cannot count on Justice.

Cid: Of course not! **There is an environment in which the thief is called "poor" and the old lady who was robbed is called a "trickster".** The killer gets out of the squad room more quickly than the policeman who arrested him. Moreover, a relentless fight against fraud, cronyism, and corruption is also absolutely crucial to the development of a Country.

Journalist: In summary, what will be the questions to ask in this case of justice?

Cid: I suggest the following questions:

Did the party, while in government
   a) favor the forces of order, creating security for the Citizen, or create a climate where one cannot go out without being robbed? (that is, did it fight crime or did it make life easier for criminals?)
   b) create a system of justice that favors the compliant Citizen, or a system of justice that facilitates life for mediocrity and the skilled crook?
   c) create the conditions for the Courts to function well, or in practice, did the Courts serve almost nothing given the time that the processes take to be resolved, and the fraudulent way many judges decide with impunity'?

These questions are interconnected, so it is also easy for the Citizen to observe how justice is doing in his Country and thus to know which parties leave the Country with a justice worthy of that name or with a miserable simulation of justice. Look at your Country. Then just vote properly.

HEALTH

Journalist: As for health, it seems to me very easy to see whether a party has governed well or not.

Cid: That's true, and we do not even need to spend much time on this topic. It is sufficient to see if hospitals and health centers are sufficient in number and have the necessary conditions to treat patients properly, if the conditions of care are good when it is necessary to go to hospitals or health centers, if health professionals (doctors, nurses ...) are valued at the same time as they are required to be responsible for dealing with human lives.

Journalist: I do not know if it seems to you that the following sums up what you said: In a Country that has been well governed, if a Citizen has a health problem, that Citizen is timely and appropriately treated in the public health services; in a Country that has been poorly governed, those who have money go to private health services, those who do not have money die at home, or they are on a waiting list, waiting for an eternity until they are called, or even tremble if they have to go to the emergency room in hospitals and health center departments due to undignified situations they have to go through, starting with the time that is necessary to wait until someone takes care of them.

Cid: That seems to me a good summary that touches the essentials for an objective choice or an objective removal of a party. As you see it is very easy to distinguish whether a party ruled well or not in this area.

Journalist: So, let us go to the issue of Social Security.

SOCIAL SECURITY

Cid: Social Security is one of the noblest functions in the organization of a society. A good Social Security system guarantees the adequate survival of the people who, because of situations unrelated to their will, cannot work for their subsistence or do not have decent living conditions.

Journalist: So how can we distinguish good from bad

governance on this subject?

Cid: We can start by checking first whether a particular party that was in government was interested in this matter. Then we need to check whether the decisions the government has made in this area were for the sake of the people who really need help or has been helping (with a view to collecting votes) parasites who do not want to work.

Journalist: But often people do not have direct access to this kind of information.

Cid: No, but we come back to the famous phrase "Cleaning begets Cleaning ..."! That is, we see what was done by the government. In bad governance there are poor people begging on the street, sometimes in a miserable state! On the other hand money is given to those who can work but stay at home getting drunk! Pensioners are given a pension that is not enough to pay for their food and medication.

Journalist: In good governance it will be the reverse ...

Cid: Yes. But in addition, good governance cuts off, for example, dinner expenses, car purchases, international visits, and all non-core expenses in order to have more money for the neediest. The situations of lack are examined with interest and objectivity by the Social Assistance, and people are helped to the extent of their needs. Living conditions are created for the disabled of any kind. This is perfectly possible, and there are Countries where it works, as in the Nordic Countries.

Journalist: Surely, in these countries, mediocrity is not in government.

Cid: Of course, but this situation did not fall from the sky. It was the Citizens who chose, and maintained, the parties that have competent rulers! And this is perfectly possible to do anywhere in the world! For that it is enough that the Citizens become conscious, as I have been insisting.

Journalist: Then, after we saw the parameters that clarify good or bad governance for us, we can go to the next step: to see the process by which we can participate in establishing the right conditions to begin the progress of a Country.

Cid: Let's go then!

SUGGESTIONS TO VOTE PROPERLY

Journalist: What are the grounds on which you based your procedure?

Cid:

First of all: The governance of a Country <u>cannot be considered a joke or a situation of personal promotion</u>. When civilized people are invited, they only choose to participate in governance if they are able to do so. But in a Country of mediocrity what matters is "to go there" and, if things go wrong, there is no problem for them because no one asks the bad rulers to take responsibility. Thus it is up to the Citizen to choose a party that seeks, maintains, and fosters honest and competent people in governance, removing the others.

In second place: The Citizen <u>must vote rationally</u>, choosing objectively by observing the state in which parties that previously ruled in his Country or in other countries have left the Country. The Citizen <u>should never vote emotionally</u>, "for the beautiful eyes" or the "speech" of some, or some party leaders, <u>nor let himself be influenced by publicity</u>. It is already known that mediocrity will paint a beautiful picture to deceive as many voters as possible. The important thing is to keep a party in government that choses intelligent-competent governors, and to remove completely the parties that have ruled the Country badly!

In third place: <u>It is necessary that the majority of voters vote for a single party</u>, so that there is no dilution of votes with the consequent rise of parties of mediocrity (because their voters for mediocrity always vote). That is why the process of choice begins by seeing if the party that was in the government should continue or be removed. If it should be removed and there is no other party that stands out positively, one must begin to apply the process of choice in the first party on the list in the principal city of the Country (As you know, the place of the parties on the voting list is drawn), because the Country may have different voting lists according to the zone of the Country, which will naturally have different party ordering and it is necessary to concentrate the votes for a single party using only the list of the principal city of the Country for this process to be effective. Then check if there is nothing against choosing this party! If there is anything that shows that the first does not serve to govern, move on to the second party... and repeat the process down the list until you find a party that serves to govern well. In this way it is possible that the majority of aware Citizens in the Country are in harmony so that there is no dilution of votes among various parties.

Journalist: Will it not complicate this process to suggest choosing the party that will appoint the rulers of a Country? Will the people with less academic education understand?

Cid: If you try it you will see that it is very simple! And there is also a figure, which illustrates the process with a general summary table to help. In short, this is a process that applies right from the beginning to the parties that have been in Parliament due to the previous elections. If they governed well (observing how education, justice, health, and social security, as presented before), vote for the main party. If these parties have ruled badly and sank the Country, do not vote for any of them, and start to apply the process of selecting the party to vote for, at the beginning of the list <u>on the ballot of the principal city of the Country</u> (because other regions of the Country may have a different party-ordering in their lists, and it is convenient to use only the ordering of a list with the objective of not diluting the votes), asking the questions presented below. If the party at the beginning of the list is not good, we continue to apply the same process to the party next on the list and so on, until we find the party for whom to vote. Very simple as you see!

Journalist: In reality it is an objective process that seeks to see well through the dust they seek us to throw in our eyes during the electoral campaigns.

Cid: That is so and anyone who follows it does not need to waste time with the election campaigns and the lies that can be said in them. What is important is to observe the previous governance, or what happened in Countries where certain parties or parties with the same ideology have already ruled. Obviously, the observation has to be global and not get stuck in only just a governation subject.

Journalist: What do you mean by that?

Cid: Do you think, for example, that a Citizen who wants to see a Country progress is going to vote for a party that calls itself "left", "right", or that is a party of religious fanatics or other fanatics, when that Citizen looks at the situation existing in the countries that were or are governed by such regimes?

Journalist: It's curious, but I had never thought about that.

Cid: Another example: if a government has made a Country progress very well, but a minister has done poorly in a particular area, does it seem wise to remove the government's party from government only because of that minister?

Journalist: In this case it seems to me that the vote should be given to this party again in the elections.

Cid: I think so too. The Prime Minister must be attentive and replace this minister before the evil gets to the other ministers if he wants to avoid the consequent removal of his party from active life in the following elections. Total perfection does not exist, but mediocrity in positions of responsibility cannot be ignored and left unaccounted for.

Journalist: And if in the elections there is not the same list for all the regions of the Country? Since the order of the parties will not be the same, the idea of having almost all the people of the Country vote for the same party will not work.

Cid: As I said before, in this case, use the ballot of the principal city of the Country and choose from that list the party to vote for according to the process presented, and then vote for that party on the list that is given, at the polling station, in the region where you will vote. So most people in the Country only vote for a party.

Journalist: But how will people know what the order of the parties is on the list of the Country's principal city?

Cid: You can check the Internet, or contact the National Election Commission that always exists in a Country. And possibly the party on the list of the Country's principal city sees that, following the process presented, it will be elected, it will do much propaganda about the list of the Country's principal city and its position in the list, for people to vote for it!

Journalist: Very well! So as to leave no doubt, it is important to make an overall, summary, as practical as possible, of the procedure: how do you start with those most voted for in the previous elections and, if they are not good, do you continue by using the list of the Country's principal city starting with the first and so on until you find the party to vote for?

Cid: Certainly! I must stress again that this process is very simple, and very powerful. Just ask yourself the sequence of linked questions that follow (a figure is also presented in the cover, which illustrates the process with a general summary table):

A) THE FIRST QUESTION: HAS THE PARTY MOST VOTED FOR IN THE PREVIOUS ELECTIONS DEVELOPED THE COUNTRY?

Check if, with the party most voted for in the previous elections, the Country has progressed in the previously described areas of health, education, justice, and Social Security, or at least kept the progress it had before in the case of a Country already developed!

If the Country has progressed: vote again for this party!

If the Country has not progressed: ask the following question (second question)

B) SECOND QUESTION: IS THERE ANY PARTY PRESENTING A PARTY PRESIDENT, SOMEONE THAT WE CAN SEE (FOR WHAT HE DID PREVIOUSLY IN LIFE) IS VALUABLE AND COMPETENT TO GOVERN THE COUNTRY?

Check if any party presents as its Leader someone who is honest (who has not been involved in fraud or corruption) with a good academic career and impeccable professional performance, having shown that he has already done something worthwhile in life and that he has chosen people of the same quality as candidates for deputies.

If there is: vote for this party!

If there is none: take the list of parties <u>on the ballot of the Country's principal city</u> (usually the lists do not have the same order of parties for the different regions of the whole Country, and it is fundamental that all people ask the following questions only in the same order of parties, so it is important to use only the list of the principal city of the Country) and ask the following questions, beginning with the first party of the Country's principal city:

C) THIRD QUESTION: HAS THIS PARTY ALREADY BEEN IN PARLIAMENT?

1- IF IT HAS BEEN ALREADY IN PARLIAMENT, then ask, has the Country progressed well in the previously described areas of health, education, justice, and Social Security, due to the party's performance while in Parliament?

If the Country has progressed: vote for this party!

If the Country has not progressed: eliminate this party and move on to the next party on the list, repeating the questions from the third. (the C)

2- IF THE PARTY HAS NOT YET BEEN IN PARLIAMENT, check if it should be removed immediately. To see that ask the following questions:

2.1- HAVE PARTIES WITH THE SAME IDEOLOGY AS THIS PARTY GOVERNED IN ANOTHER COUNTRY?

2.1.1- If they have already ruled in another Country, has that Country evolved very well in the previously described areas of health, education, justice, and Social

Security, or have they destroyed that Country?

> - If they have evolved that Country, vote for that party!

> - If they have destroyed that Country, go to the next party on the list and repeat the questions from the third. (the C)

2.1.2- If they did not govern in another Country, is the ideology of that party for the progress of Civilization, or for lies, for fanaticism, and for the angry destruction of adversaries?

> - If it is for the progress of Civilization: vote for that party!

> -If it is for lies, for fanaticism, and for the raging destruction of the opponents, just abandon this party, go to the next party on the list and repeat the questions from the third. (the C)

> - If it is impossible to know the ideology of that party, check, as far as possible (for example checking on the Internet) if the main people of that party and if the people it proposes for deputies are serious people with character and have already done something good in their lives.

> > - If they are, vote for that party;

> > - If they are not, go to the next party on the list and repeat the questions from the third. (the C)

Journalist: In fact it seems easy!

Cid: And it's very easy! If people try, they will see that this procedure gives good results. As you can see, if this process is systematically used in elections, political mediocrity will begin to disappear and parties will endeavor to enlist intelligent and competent people. This process only fails if people do not follow it, that is, if they get caught in a problem.

Journalist: And what is this problem?

Cid: A problem appears if people fail to follow the proposed questions and begin to think emotionally, like "I always voted for party A, so I do not feel good if I change my party" or "At my home everyone votes for party B, so I also have to vote for party B", or even "candidate X is very friendly and has appealing conversation; maybe I will vote for his party (even if that candidate is a professional nobody)". Or if people start thinking, "They are all the same. I'm already fed up with this, and so I'm not going to vote, or I am going to vote 'abstain' or blank". You see the situation: people stop being rational, they get emotional or are led by the "vicar's tale" and false promises that may appear in election campaigns, voting badly or failing to vote, and the Country continues to be ruled by parasitic "ticks" continuing to sink the Country!

Journalist: But there will always be people of this kind, or ignorant people who are cheated and vote badly.

Cid: Of course there will always be people of this kind, but if they are half a dozen, that's okay. The problem arises when most people do not vote or vote badly!

Journalist: And often bad governors also come into office because of abstention. People are increasingly not going to vote because they stopped believing in politicians.

Cid: That is why I told you earlier that abstention can

become the main cause of the sinking of a Country in mediocrity. With the new process described above, each Citizen must vote, but vote well, and being a voting Citizen is helping to clean up the "political garbage" by eliminating the parties that live with mediocrity. Thus, instead of abstaining, they have the opportunity to use the list on the ballot of the Country's principal city to vote massively for a single party, giving it the majority and making the others that sank the Country disappear. On the other hand, the party that won the elections with this new process already knows that if it does not govern to develop the Country and improve people's living conditions, in the next elections they will be eliminated from the political scene.

Journalist: Yes, in reality the main problem appears when the same parties are always "there", whether they govern well or govern poorly.

Cid: You see: What goes through the head of someone who thinks, and acts consciously, to abstain or to vote again for a party that has made a Country sink and remain in misery? It is necessary to be very stupid!

Journalist: It is evident that for the Country to develop, such a party should be removed. But often people say there are no others good parties, or that they are all the same.

Cid: As I said before, this is what mediocre parties want people to think. I repeat: if in the elections people do not abstain and follow the question process presented earlier, the parties of mediocrity disappear from political life (the "ticks" are pulled out), and the party that is elected is already warned that it will disappear if it does not govern well. On the other hand, do not forget that "mediocrity" always votes to keep those who support it.

Journalist: But all that you have said is like causing a revolution in a Country!

Cid: It's not a revolution! It's an Evolution! This is what any Country needs. Moreover, in the beginning, the Citizen owes nothing to politicians. The politicians are the ones who owe the Citizens for being treated as "Honorable Member" or "Minister", living at the expense of our taxes! If they do not fulfill their function, with ability, with dedication, and with honesty, they must be removed without thinking about it!

Journalist: What about the so-called protest vote in the opposition party?

Cid: If people only vote for a party of the so-called opposition because they feel revolted by the performance of another party, they run the risk of blindly voting and bringing into power a party that has previously ruled poorly. This is what is commonly called "coming out of the frying pan into the fire". And the Country becomes even worse! Following the question sequence avoids this!

Journalist: And if people vote to abstain?

Cid: It is an expenditure of pure energy for nothing. In practice they simply appear in statistics, but it does not change anything. What counts are the votes for the parties. The process that I presented you has the same energy expenditure (to go to vote), but it is effective in moving out mediocrity and maintaining competence in governance.

Journalist: Now it seems clear to me why the Countries Advanced in Civilization seek to have the best people in places of governance. Check what happens, for example, in the Nordic Countries!

Cid: Neither more nor less! Only in this way can a Country evolve! Finally, and again, do not forget that "mediocrity" always votes. Citizens who want to create and live in an evolved Country can not let "mediocrity" choose for themselves, which is what happens if they do not vote. It is fatal for the development of a Country that a party that has ruled poorly continues to have deputies in parliament, even if it is in the so-called opposition.

Journalist: It is curious that at the end of our conversation, I get the feeling that what you said is part of common sense.

Cid: It's common sense! It is only necessary that people use it, and do not let it go during the discussions by experts or snobs. Do you remember the history of Columbus' egg? *The most ludicrous thing of all is that there is a real possibility of changing a Country, and people do not do it !!!* And as simple as drinking a glass of water: it is enough to go, on election day, to make a little cross on the ballot rationally (not emotionally), in the right place. So does it not seem incredible to you that sometimes people let the Country sink by not going to vote? Is it not amazing how a small action can change so much for the better ... or worse? That is why the Citizen has to be conscious and active!

Journalist: Now, all I have to do is to thank you for the time you have devoted to this subject, hoping that people will make this small effort to go vote on election day and vote rationally for the good of all!

Cid: You're welcome! It was a pleasure because it is the function of a Citizen worthy of that name to naturally try to make Civilization and the environment where he lives evolve. Now all that's necessary is that people try it to see that it works, so they can have a Country where it's good to live. And this will only happen when people start thinking about these things by themselves!

THE "ARISTODEMOCRACY"

AN INCREASE IN THE "LEVEL OF CIVILIZATION"!

The process presented previously for the choice of a party to govern a Country is the first and fundamental step for the development of a Country if it is mired in a governance of mediocrity: clean up that mediocrity. Then it is necessary to create an automatic system (free of graft) that allows only the most intelligent-competent people with the highest level of Civilization to be allowed to be the future rulers. This avoids the sad spectacle of a Country having a Parliament formed by acephalous beings who vote as a "herd" with all of the same color to vote the same way, like a colored robot, seeking the self-interest or the interest of the party, instead of trying to make the Country evolve.

Have you really noticed the "work" of the Parliament, or the Assembly of the Republic, or any other name for all the Members elected in a system of mediocrity? To the questions, "Who votes in favor?" the blue robots rise; "Who votes against?" the red robots rise; "Who abstains?" the orange robots rise (or any other color composition that the reader wants to consider!). Isn't it cheaper for this Country if, instead of spending money on " robot people," their drivers and stewards, they would buy colored puppets of wood that could be installed in Parliament and were controlled by a switch in the party headquarters of the same color, switch the one that made the colored wooden puppets with the color raised at the time of the polls? Is this rising and sitting, according to the color of the party, the work of a competent deputy? Would a competent Parliament not have the proposals submitted approved by more than 90% of the deputies, if they were good for the Country, or rejected by more than 90% if those proposals are not good for the Country? After all, is what matters the color of the party or the Country?

Here is a story to better illustrate the governance situation by incompetent people. Imagine that you had a heart attack and are being taken to the operating table in the hospital, when an employee arrives and says to you, "Today the cardiologist had a problem and can not come, but do not worry because we have already made an election and we chose the cleaning maid to operate you, because she is very friendly and speaks very well!" How would you feel if that happened? Would a hospital let an incompetent person operate? It does not make any sense, does it? So does it seem to make any sense to be able to vote for an incompetent person or a crook to govern a Country, as is currently possible in most of the so-called democratic countries? It is obvious that any Country will sink with such rulers! Just see what has happened in your own countries!

Aristodemocracy avoids these situations by allowing only intelligent, competent, and therefore honest people to have access to the positions of governance! It is these kinds of people who can advance a Country when implementing the system of Aristodemocracy. And when implemented, it is beneficial for all!

IT WILL TAKE TIME AND REQUIRE EFFORT, BUT IT'S WORTH IT!

The process of implementation of Aristodemocracy that will be presented next does not take place overnight, as is the case with all that is worthwhile: first, it requires that it be understood and assimilated; then it requires time and effort not to give up or fall into the temptation of taking advantage of the system for personal benefit (do not forget that the implementation of the system is what brings real benefit to all). But it is simple and, as you can see, we will remain at another Level of Civilization: education as it should be, a Country without poor people, free health without waiting lines, health care by competent doctors who were trained by serious education. People are paid according to their type of responsibility and not by their "antics" or by the party to which they belong.

Do you think that this is impossible? That would be to think wrong! It is perfectly possible to do and even very simple to implement! But of course, if most people think it's impossible and get stuck with "it's always been like this and it always will be," and they do not do what is necessary, namely going to vote well, then such a civilized society will not happen!

Here is a story to illustrate the situation in which most people trapped in mediocrity live in chains that only exist in their imagination and are fueled by brainwashing advertising:

«A merchant went with his camel caravan through the desert and it was necessary to camp for the night. The servants came to him saying, "We have a problem because we only brought 9 stakes to tie 10 camels". He responds, "There's no problem! The camels are stupid animals, so tie the 9 camels to the stakes, and when you reach the one who does not have a stake, pretend to bury a stake and tie it to an imaginary stake. He will remain unmoved, like the others, even without being tied!" The servants did that, and the camel was there bound to the imaginary stake, without leaving, like the others. The next day, the servants hurried back to the merchant, very distressed, saying, "We do not know what's going on. All the camels are ready to continue their journey, except the one who had no stake; he won't move!" The merchant answered them, "Have you ever made the gestures of untying him, as if he were really tied?" They said, "We did not even remember that". They then made the gestures of untying the camel bound with an imaginary rope to the imaginary stake, and he went on his way with the others! »

This is how most people behave in life, tied to the behaviors that mediocrity created to keep people "tied" to what is fashionable, to the party they have always voted for, etc., … without thinking for themselves and acting rationally!

And don't you think it's worth it to make an effort to become free, to start thinking for yourself, and to implement the regime of Civilized Society in a Country?

THE "CORE IDEA"

The basic idea of Aristodemocracy, presented below, is so evident that it does not even seem necessary to present it. But I challenge the reader to find a single Country where it is really and institutionally implemented.

As is easily seen, any organization or service only progresses if it has competent people to perform the tasks in which they have competence. As we have seen before, no one would normally like to have their appendix operated on by the hospital's cleaning maid, but only by a doctor who has the competence to do so. She has to be competent in her cleaning service, and that's how things go well!

It is therefore no wonder that *for a Country to develop, and its Citizens to live well, it must not be any "smart guy" who governs, but rather the people who are the most intelligent, competent, honest (civilized), and interested in helping others who must ensure the governance of a Country in the areas in which they are competent.* This is the basic idea of Aristodemocracy, the system proposed to implement the "core idea". Then everything else runs on wheels!

HOW TO DO THIS?

The fundamental question then arises: How does the society managed under the Aristodemocracy system find out if a person is intelligent, competent, honest, and interested in helping others enough to become a ruler? And how do you prevent the mediocre son of a friend of the President from being able to be nominated for a management position, just because he is the son of the President's friend?

The process is very easy to implement, as long as people want it, and begins in primary school: every teacher knows among his students who the smart, the honest, the friends, are and also who the "others" are…! So, just set up an individual registration!

The same would happen in secondary and higher education. Thus, upon finishing university each student would already have his or her "behavioral, civilizational, and skills mark" registered since Primary School.

In this way, the civilized society would already have the data it needs to know if a given person can contribute to governance in order to make the Country evolve, or if he is a liar who claims to be a boss. It is therefore enough to have an honest record of the skills and the character of each student from Primary School and not only of their classifications as it is done currently. (And there could also be a record of the actions of the parents who tried to have the teacher hide the child's real situation with a higher grade than the one due to the child, because "the son of a fish knows how to swim," and we would already have indications of fraudulent education at home.)

Then the same would happen in the professional "curriculum" and then we could just use that record to make Aristodemocracy work well: a party will only choose and only present, to govern the Country, people who are sufficiently intelligent, competent, honest and interested in helping others!

THE FUNCTIONING OF ARISTODEMOCRACY

Aristodemocracy must be rooted in the fundamental principles of honesty and altruism: a "dishonest " and a selfish person must be excluded from governance right from the start! An anti-fraud system that is present in all structures of social organization must therefore be set up right from the start.

So to speak, from the cradle the Citizen of this evolved Country has to breathe honesty, seeing and feeling that any attempt at fraud puts him in a worse position than if he had behaved honestly, and with dire consequences for his life.

In summary, the idea that "crime does not pay", but rather honesty, really needs to be perfectly clear and operational. As an example, in a Country with Aristodemocracy it doesn't even occur to a student to copy to get a good grade, because he knows from the beginning that he has to study and know the subject.

It is absolutely fundamental that crooks, and those who are corrupt, inhuman, and "skillful" in lies cannot reach places of leadership!

Then, in the elections, people that are presenting

themselves for positions of governance must have a transparent history revealing their competence for the position of government that they seek, perfectly transparent for the other Citizens who are going to vote, so that they can vote consciously and well informed about the kind of people a party presents to govern!

DO NOT FALL ASLEEP WITH THE ROUTINE

Once Aristodemocracy is implemented, it has to be taken care of. Mediocrity always seeks new ways of overcoming Competence (instead of trying to destroy Competence, mediocrity should try to become Competence for the good of all). Thus one can not "fall asleep at the wheel": the government of the Country governed by Aristodemocracy must ensure that this regime continues and take care that the mediocre, the selfish, and those who live by appearances do not assume leading positions. That is why it can never be assumed that everything is automatically ensured; the workings of Aristodemocracy, for example, can be dislodged by allowing the friend's son to occupy a position for which he has no competence!

On the other hand, the government of the Country governed by Aristodemocracy must encourage by all means the development of the qualities of each person, which are different from person to person but are all useful for the different areas of action in the Country. *The fundamental thing is not to want to be or to seem better than others, <u>but to be honest and to develop one's own capacities</u> without comparing them with those of others but putting one's own capacities to the service of the common good!*

HOPE NEVER DIES!

As the reader can see, the implementation of Aristodemocracy is very simple and perfectly executable, and it places the Country on a level of Civilization where human beings would like to live.

But this regime does not "fall from the sky" and will not appear in one day! Even if others around you cannot see their usefulness soon, do not give up or lose Hope. Try to enlighten the people in your life as much as possible, and ask those who can understand to help Humanity evolve by talking about this system to other people. The process will thus be publicized and will open a door of Hope to the disillusioned with this policy showing them a simple way that can be put into practice! So people will grow in Civilization and this regime will be quickly implemented throughout the world.

As you can imagine, when this system of Aristodemocracy will be implemented in the world, there will be no people starving and no abnormal people to generate wars! And each person will look at other people who pass through life as friendly people and will enjoy living!

www.ingramcontent.com/pod-product-compliance
Lightning Source LLC
Chambersburg PA
CBHW051413250726
48655CB00003B/1018